GRASSHOPPERS

INSECTS

James P. Rowan

The Rourke Corporation, Inc.
Vero Beach, Florida 32964

Edited by Sandra A. Robinson

PHOTO CREDITS
© Lynn M. Stone: cover, title page, pages 4, 8, 12, 15, 18, 21;
© Breck Kent: page 7; © James P. Rowan: pages 10, 12; © Barry
Mansell: page 17.

Library of Congress Cataloging-in-Publication Data

Rowan, James P.
   Grasshoppers / by James P. Rowan.
      p.   cm. — (Insects)
   Includes index.
   Summary: Explores the world of grasshoppers, discussing where
they live, how they grow up, what they eat, and other insects related
to them.
   ISBN 0-86593-286-7
   1. Grasshoppers—Juvenile literature. [1. Grasshoppers.]
I. Title. II. Series.
QL508.A2S86   1993
595.7'26—dc20   93-7586
                                                                    CIP
                                                                     AC

TABLE OF CONTENTS

GRASSHOPPERS

Grasshoppers are the kangaroos of the insect kingdom. With their large, powerful hind legs, grasshoppers can sometimes leap away from their enemies to safety.

Grasshoppers have large heads, too, and strong jaws that allow them to eat tough plants.

Grasshoppers have six legs. Most **species,** or kinds, of grasshoppers have two pairs of wings. The hind wings fold up like fans against the grasshopper's body when it is resting.

Tiny leg barbs give grasshoppers a grip on grass

KINDS OF GRASSHOPPERS

Over 600 species of grasshoppers live in North America. One of the largest, the colorful lubber, never grows wings as an adult.

Red-legged grasshoppers are common in the Midwest. They live in fields and grasslands. They become pests when they feed on farm crops.

Many common grasshopper species belong to a group known as spur-throated grasshoppers.

Face-to-face with a spur-throated grasshopper

KATYDIDS

Katydids are among the most colorful grasshoppers. Many are long, narrow and green, like the grass where they hide.

Katydids are sometimes called long-horned grasshoppers. The "horns" are the two whiplike **antennas** that are on the katydid's head.

It is easier to hear a katydid than to see one. Like most grasshoppers, katydids have colors that match their surroundings. They are well-hidden, or **camouflaged.** However, their loud clicking or buzzing sounds give them away.

*An unusual pink katydid at home
on a grass-pink orchid*

9

OTHER GRASSHOPPER COUSINS

Grasshoppers belong to a group of chewing insects that includes many interesting members. Crickets, for example, use special wing parts to produce loud, chirping sounds.

Another grasshopper cousin, the walkingstick, is an amazing **mimic.** It looks like a twig with legs! Walkingsticks live in trees and munch on leaves.

Mantises have a more unusual diet than other grasshopper relatives. They use their jaws to prey upon other insects—including grasshoppers.

The praying mantis stalks insects, including its grasshopper cousins

The walkingstick blends beautifully with real sticks

A katydid in Costa Rica mimics a dead leaf

WHERE GRASSHOPPERS LIVE

All grasshoppers eat **vegetation,** or plants. Almost everywhere that plants grow, grasshoppers live. They live and feed in gardens, fields and deserts. Many kinds live in tropical rain forests, too.

Some grasshoppers eat only certain kinds of plants. These grasshoppers must live where the plants grow. Grasshoppers that eat many different plants can live in more places.

Blades of grass — a grasshopper's quiet, but dangerous kingdom

A GRASSHOPPER GROWS UP

Each fall a female grasshopper lays her eggs in a tiny burrow in the soil.

Young grasshoppers hatch in spring. They are called **nymphs.** A grasshopper nymph looks like a tiny adult grasshopper, but it does not have wings.

As a nymph grows, it sheds—it slips out of its outer skin. It may shed up to eight times. After the final shed, it is an adult.

A katydid nymph
steps out — of its skin!

PREDATORS AND PREY

Because there are so many grasshoppers, they are **prey,** or food, for many kinds of insect hunters, or **predators.** Birds such as gulls, screech owls, blackbirds and small hawks eat grasshoppers. Toads, frogs, snakes, foxes, coyotes and skunks eat grasshoppers, too. And the grasshopper mouse earned its name by filling up on the insect!

Grasshoppers can spit a liquid—sometimes called "tobacco juice"—to scare predators. It's messy stuff, but it doesn't frighten many grasshopper enemies.

Caught in a sticky web, the grasshopper becomes spider prey

GRASSHOPPER PLAGUES

Grasshoppers usually feed alone or in small groups. Certain kinds, however, form huge swarms with millions of grasshoppers.

These swarms move across the land and eat each bit of vegetation in their path. When large numbers of grasshoppers destroy crops, they are called **plagues.**

Grasshopper plagues struck western America in the 1800s. They still happen in Asia and Africa from time to time.

Grasshoppers aren't a problem until one is joined by one million more

GRASSHOPPERS AND PEOPLE

Most species of grasshoppers are not plentiful enough to cause major crop damage. However, some kinds do occasionally cause serious problems with gardens and food crops.

When grasshoppers in large numbers become pests, they damage millions of dollars worth of crops. In addition, millions of dollars are spent on poisons used to kill them.

Glossary

antennas (an TEN uhz) — whiplike structures on the heads of insects and several other boneless animals

camouflage (KAM o flahj) — to hide by matching an animal's color to its surroundings

nymph (NIMPF) — a stage in the life of a young insect; the young of certain insects

plague (PLAYG) — widespread damage, often caused by great numbers of insects

predator (PRED uh tor) — an animal that kills other animals for food

prey (PRAY) — an animal that is hunted for food by another animal

species (SPEE sheez) — within a group of closely-related animals, such as grasshoppers, one certain kind or type (*differential* grasshopper)

vegetation (vehdg eh TAY shun) — plants; the covering of plant life on a surface

INDEX